Original title:
Searching for Meaning in the Comfort of Bed

Copyright © 2025 Creative Arts Management OÜ
All rights reserved.

Author: Ophelia Ravenscroft
ISBN HARDBACK: 978-1-80566-240-2
ISBN PAPERBACK: 978-1-80566-535-9

Daybreak Discoveries

Pillow peaks of fluffy dreams,
I dive into the fabric seams.
Lost in twirls of twisted sheets,
Who knew breakfast could be defeat?

Tattered Corners of Thought

Underneath the bed's embrace,
Dust bunnies make a silly chase.
Thick with crumbs from late-night treats,
My mind takes breaks like lazy beats.

The Feathered Plateau of Reflection

Cushioned scenes in morning light,
I ponder life, or maybe bites.
Feathered dreams take off and fly,
Yet still my coffee's run awry.

Whispers Beneath the Threadbare Canopy

Softly I scheme 'neath threads so worn,
Heroic battles I bet are sworn.
Shadows dance in morning play,
But all my socks just run away.

Whispers Beneath the Blankets

Beneath the layers, secrets lie,
A sock's lost wisdom, a pillow's sigh.
The dust bunnies plot, they're quite a crew,
Scheming their escape to find the loo.

Cereal crumbs dance in the moonlight,
While fuzzy slippers conspire in fright.
The bedpost listens, it takes great cheer,
To hear the tales whispered loud and clear.

The Thrum of Thoughts at Dawn

Morning light creeps in, full of cheer,
While thoughts tumble in, a raucous sphere.
Would breakfast harmonize with my dream?
Or does toast and jam just ruin the theme?

Pillows play host to my wildest schemes,
As I ponder life over half-closed beams.
The thermostat creaks, 'Hey, stay in bed!'
But my thoughts are racing, full steam ahead.

Dreams Cradle the Weary Soul

In slumber's clutch, my mind takes flight,
Where cats and hats hold a grand delight.
A dragon in slippers, all plump and sweet,
   Offers me cookies as a breakfast treat.

The clock ticks softly, a lullaby's tune,
While I've sworn to conquer the sun and moon.
Yet here I lay, wrapped in feathery bliss,
   Chasing odd dreams, like a hit-or-miss.

In the Warmth of Woven Threads

Threads of comfort, woven so tight,
Keep out the chill with each cozy night.
My blanket's a fortress, my bed a retreat,
Where adventures abound without missing a beat.

The thermostat snickers, it knows my plight,
Turning warm nights into a joyous sight.
The alarm clock growls, its time to behave,
Yet here I remain, like a wise little knave.

The Language of Dreams and Duvets

In my quilted fortress, I lay,
Pillow armies march to play.
Teacup castles made of fluff,
Whispered secrets, never tough.

Under covers, worlds collide,
Socks and pillows, dreams abide.
Funny faces creep and roam,
Atop this mattress, I'm alone.

Monsters made of comfort food,
Dance around, they're in the mood.
Tacos singing lullabies,
Who knew food could hypnotize?

Lost in nonsense, sleep's embrace,
Pajama parties, silly space.
In the land of snores and sighs,
My bed's a haven, oh, so wise.

Lanterns of Light in a Darkened Room

Glow of screens, my midnight friends,
They talk and giggle, never end.
Flashlight beams like lantern sprites,
Illuminating pillow fights.

Rummaging through dreams of cheese,
A fondue fountain, if you please.
Under sheets, my mind's a show,
Juggling thoughts like pros at pro.

Bedtime snacks are calling me,
Whisked away in mystery.
Teddy bears with wise old eyes,
Whisper truths in muffled sighs.

Lights flicker, shadows prance,
In this weird, nocturnal dance.
With giggles echoing, I swoon,
Lanterns spark till morning's noon.

Unraveling Knots of Day's Dilemmas

Tangled sheets, today's last fight,
Decisions wrestle in the night.
Should I snooze or should I bake?
Dreaming of a giant cake?

Questions swarm like buzzing bees,
Poking fun at life with ease.
Laundry's singing, "Fold me now!"
I just giggle; no, not how!

Each dilemma's a playful jest,
As socks compete for bed's best nest.
Sorting worries, what a task,
I beg the night, "Just let me bask!"

With pillow fights and laughter bright,
I chase away the tense moonlight.
Morning comes, my thoughts still swell,
To bed I go, for all is well.

Whirls of Yearning Underneath the Stars

Under blankets, dreams take flight,
Whirls of chaos greet the night.
Counting stars, I start to roam,
My bed transformed to cosmic home.

Spaceships made of crumpled sheets,
Astronauts in mismatched feets.
Galaxies of snacks abound,
Galaxy quests spun all around.

Wishing wells in murky dreams,
Sipping on my chocolate creams.
Comets made of candy bars,
Zooming 'round, we play with stars.

In this universe of fluff,
I find my goofy self enough.
So here I lay, my laughter gleams,
In whirls of yearning, chasing dreams.

Embracing the Ether

In my cocoon, I ponder and dream,
Why does the alarm clock always scream?
Beneath my covers, I laugh and sigh,
Should I rise, or just stay and lie?

Pajamas snug in a tangled mess,
The remote's lost, I must confess.
Each thought flits by like a wayward fly,
Is it too early to bid time goodbye?

Coffee brews, but I ponder the cup,
"Maybe five more minutes?" I only sit up.
A snack in hand, oh, blissful delight,
Who knew deep thoughts could start with a bite?

Wrapped in warmth, no need to race,
Making peace with this cozy space.
Maybe tomorrow, I'll venture out,
But today, I cherish the lazy clout.

Cuddled in Questions

Curled up tight, what's life's big call?
Do socks have feelings if they fall?
My pillow knows all my best-kept tales,
As I drift between naps and hilarious fails.

The world outside hums an urgent tune,
But here I'm a lazy afternoon cartoon.
With crumbs in my bed, I start to scheme,
Perhaps I'll invent a new napping dream.

Reality's fog can be quite absurd,
Especially when cats when meow like birds.
If I had a dollar for each thought I had,
I could fund my quest for the ultimate fad.

Yet here I remain, a whimsical ghost,
Navigating humor, my daily toast.
In this fortress of fabric, how can I win?
When becoming a legend feels like a sin!

Blanketed by Uncertainty

Underneath layers, both soft and bright,
What's for dinner? Leftovers or a bite?
Questions abound like stars in the night,
All I can tell is that I feel just right.

The fridge might ooze with last week's glee,
But right now, it's just the cat and me.
If thoughts were cookies, I'd surely bake,
Imposing my will upon each little shake.

Should I join the world or stay tucked away?
What's the real difference? Why not sway?
To laugh or to cry, it's all quite the game,
In quilts of confusion, I'll still find my fame.

The clock ticks away, but so what, oh dear?
For here in cocoon, I hold all I fear.
With snacks and with dreams, I'll kick back and jest,
For life from the covers is truly the best!

In the Arms of Hibernation

Under these sheets, I'm a bear with pride,
Dreaming of honey as I gently glide.
Should I surf the net or nap for a bit?
Does 'hibernate' mean to fully commit?

Blanketed snug in this fluffy embrace,
Where worries dissolve and there's no such race.
Outside the wind howls, it sings me a tune,
But here, I'm a legend, a comfy cocoon.

Pixels glow bright; they tease and entice,
Yet under my duvet, everything's nice.
A world of chaos, like socks lost in fate,
But my kingdom of quilts can patiently wait.

So I'll toast to the day with a giggle or two,
To being a champion of naps overdue.
In the arms of slumber, I'll reign as king,
For nothing feels finer than what pillows bring!

In Slumber's Embrace

Under blankets thick as clouds,
I declare a war against my thoughts.
But pillows whisper soft and loud,
Inviting me to tie these knots.

With each yawn, my dreams take flight,
Chasing after socks long gone.
The fridge's hum becomes my nightlight,
But snacks will have to wait till dawn.

In this nest, I plot and scheme,
To solve life's puzzle, piece by piece.
Yet all that comes is a silly dream,
Where penguins dance and worries cease.

So here I'll stay, and laugh a bit,
With cozy warmth and fuzzy feet.
The world can wait; I'll just sit,
In slumber's arms, so snug and neat.

Thoughts Drift Like Feathers

In a realm where shadows prance,
My mind does flips and silly dives.
As daytime frowns, I find my chance,
To swim in thoughts like happy hives.

Pajamas hug me like a tune,
As daydreams chase the moonlit beams.
I ponder if I'll float to June,
Or just be lost in endless memes.

With popcorn clouds, I craft my show,
Where socks and spoons engage in fights.
Each giggle echoes soft and low,
In whispers of my cozy nights.

So here I float, a feathered sprite,
On pillows plush, I seek my fun.
With every chuckle, day turns bright,
Until the morning's final run.

Chasing Shadows of Clarity

In this soft cocoon I dwell,
Thoughts bounce like balls of yarn in play.
What's big and bold I cannot tell,
As naps become my grand ballet.

Between the sheets, I stalk my fears,
Like cats that pounce on shadows cast.
With laughter breaking through the tears,
I find my joys, both slow and fast.

Why ponder life's perplexing maze?
When I can feast on cereal crumbs?
In pillow fort, I spend my days,
While ticking clocks play silly drums.

A kingdom built from cozy dreams,
Where nothing's serious, all absurd.
I ride the waves of giggly streams,
As clarity's a fleeting bird.

Between the Stitching of Time

A quilt of thoughts wraps round my head,
Where silly jokes and shadows meet.
In moonlit corners, dreams are fed,
As socks collaborate with my feet.

What's out there looms, a distant fuss,
Yet here, I'm king of cozy realms.
With laughter bubbling, I make a fuss,
And twirl away my daily overwhelms.

Each tick-tock giggles in its race,
While I hold court with dust bunnies.
Life's worries vanish without a trace,
Replaced by quirky pillow punnies.

In this sanctuary of delight,
Time pauses, bends, and laughs with me.
So let the world spin out of sight,
As I bask in jest, so wild and free.

When Solitude Breeds Enlightenment

In the quiet hour just past the dusk,
Blanket fortress wrapped in soft husk,
I ponder deep thoughts, then laugh with glee,
At the sock monster lurking near me.

The ceiling spins with tales untold,
Was that a shadow? Or just the fold?
With each twist and turn, I set my mind,
On pizza toppings, oh what a find!

In dreams, I dance with popcorn stars,
Chasing wild ducks, riding in cars,
Thoughts converge and float about,
Who knew my brain could twist and flout?

As I yawn wide and scratch my head,
The thoughts pile up like crumbs in bed,
It's clear as day as I lay so free,
The universe laughs right back at me.

A Patchwork of Restless Wonder.

Underneath this grand quilt maze,
Thoughts tumble and trip in a fuzzy daze,
What if cats ruled and dogs wore shoes?
Oh, the hilarity—I just can't choose!

The clock ticks louder, it's now or never,
A comedy show with no end, clever,
My sleepy brain calls out for a snack,
Not another epiphany, bring me some mac!

Memories whirl like socks in a dryer,
Who stole my dreams, oh mischievous buyer?
In this patchwork kingdom, I reign supreme,
With marshmallow clouds, I dare to dream.

But when sunlight creeps, all thoughts turn bland,
Reality bites; I must understand,
Yet here I lay, and let laughter spread,
Tomorrow's questions can wait in bed.

Dreams Cradled in Cotton

In this soft boat made of luscious thread,
I sail through giggles without a shred,
With gummy bears as my starry crew,
Each wave a chuckle, oh what a view!

I jive with clouds, they're funny, I swear,
Why do they float without a care?
Each snooze is a ride on an uncharted sea,
With jellybean fish that dance just for me.

The morning light is a raucous alarm,
Yet I fumble with dreams—what a charm!
Who knew my pillows, so fluffy and white,
Could host such banter all through the night?

But as sunlight breaks the cozy retreat,
The laughter fades, feels bittersweet,
Yet I'll return, for I've learned a lot,
In this cotton cradle where dreams swirl and rot.

The Pillow's Gentle Whisper

Oh pillow, speak sweet words to my ear,
Tell me jokes that only you can hear,
As I nestle in your plush embrace,
The giggles echo, lightens the space.

Every fold a secret, every fluff a tale,
In this whimsical world, I gently sail,
Where moody ducks wear fashionable hats,
And sleepy cats hold debates with bats.

With every snore, I conjure a plot,
About a toaster that thinks it's hot,
Each chuckle bubbles, as I drift away,
To lands of whimsy where laughter will stay.

Yet alas, dawn breaks; my giggles retreat,
The pillow sighs, admitting defeat,
But I'll be back to share more delight,
Dreams are just jokes that tickle the night.

Driftwood Dreams

Beneath my sheets, the world feels small,
Where fluff and pillows beckon my call.
A land of donuts, ice cream galore,
Adventures waiting just behind the door.

With every snore, a new tale unfolds,
I'm King of the Castle, or so it is told.
Every snack's a feast, I munch and I chew,
In this cozy realm where the wild dreams brew.

The Search for Light in the Dark

In shadows cast by nighttime's embrace,
I ponder life's meaning, but it's hard to chase.
A sock on my face and a pillow so plump,
How can one think when ensconced in the lump?

Monsters lurk under my warm, cozy quilt,
But they're just my thoughts, wrapped up in guilt.
I reach for the lamp, to illuminate fate,
Tripping on slippers, it's truly first-rate.

Wrapped in Soft Contentment

Underneath layers of softness I sink,
In a kingdom where even the GMT can blink.
The clock ticks away, but who really cares?
With snacks in my lap, I'm free from all snares.

A sea of duvet, a fortress of fluff,
Every problem outside – too big and too tough.
But here in this bubble, the world fades away,
With dreams on a platter, I'm happy to stay.

The Hidden Lessons of Linen

Linen whispers secrets when the night is still,
Such as 'don't forget to eat your last meal!'
In the twilight hours, wisdom grips tight,
Like 'don't sleep without checking the fridge tonight!'

Every rumpled wrinkle holds tales from the past,
Of socks that ran away, way too fast.
The magic of sheets, it's plain to see,
They cradle my chaos, they just let me be.

Stars Beneath the Feathered Sky

Under blankets snug and tight,
I ponder life with all my might.
The stars outside, they twinkle bright,
But here it's me, a comfy sight.

With every yawn, a dream I weave,
In pillow talk, I dare believe.
Cereal boxes whisper low,
A cosmos in my room's sweet glow.

Doodles dance across my mind,
As I search for snacks, the rarest kind.
Oh, this bed, my throne so grand,
In this realm, I rule the land.

So flip and flop, the night goes on,
With silly thoughts till break of dawn.
The universe, it fits so well,
In my cocoon, where thoughts can swell.

The Land of Muffled Musings

In my fortress made of sheets,
I dodge the world, and crave more treats.
The clock ticks loudly, yet I lay,
In this blissful world, I want to stay.

Imagine penguins in a dance,
While I contemplate my next big chance.
Do socks belong on both my feet?
Or is it freedom to be incomplete?

Napping's art, I've mastered well,
In dreams, I often cast my spell.
With whirling thoughts, I roam afar,
Yet never move, just dream and spar.

The walls are lined with laughter's glow,
As I concoct my next great show.
A pillow fight with my own head,
In this land, I fear no dread.

When Night Paints the Walls with Hopes

With walls that smile in shadows cast,
I drift in dreams, a night so vast.
The stars flap wings and come to play,
While I sip cocoa, calling it a day.

Each thought a raindrop on my mind,
A jumble of wishes all intertwined.
What if cats could speak, I muse,
And tell us secrets they would choose?

Blanket forts hide my wild schemes,
Where candy rains and laughter beams.
The moon hangs low, a cheeky glee,
As it listens in on fantasies.

Oh, what wonders lie in wait,
In this cozy room, I participate.
With giggles wrapped in flannel folds,
The best of dreams, at night, unfolds.

Cocooned in a Universe of Thoughts

Tucked in tight like a burrito,
My mind's a carnival, quite a show!
Who knew a bed could hold such fun?
Inventing worlds where wild dreams run.

Each giggle echoes through the night,
While squirrels debate in a laughable fight.
The ceiling's a canvas, my weirdo spree,
Imagination's best, no end to see!

Lazily I plot each silly prank,
Should I leave my socks in the kitchen tank?
Oh, the joy of mischief in cozy quarters,
While munching on those bedtime hoarders!

With every sigh, new fancies bloom,
In this chrysalis, my worries zoom.
Wrapped in laughter, I take my flight,
In this universe, I own the night.

Hiding in the Warmth of Thought

Beneath the covers, I dive and roll,
Dreaming of tacos and a giant mole.
In pillow forts, I reign supreme,
Deciding which snack is my grandest dream.

With a quilt as my cape, I'm a hero at rest,
Conquering crumbs, yes, I'm truly blessed.
The world outside can wait a while,
I'll ponder why socks disappear in style.

Blankets wrinkle, stories unfold,
Whispered secrets, a million untold.
I find the laughter in every snore,
My mind's on vacation, who could want more?

So send me a cosmos or pie in the sky,
As I lounge like a cat, you can hear my sly sigh.
Each thought a noodle, whimsically caught,
In this fortress of giggles, I plan my plot.

The Lullaby of Contemplation

Cuddled in fluff, my ideas take flight,
Should I get up or just nap tonight?
The clock ticks softly, a lullaby sound,
As deep thoughts bubble, then splat on the ground.

Do I really need pants? That's quite the debate,
As I contemplate life in this cozy state.
A snack-sized dilemma, should it be cheese,
Or a slice of cake that will bring me to knees?

Fluffy clouds drift in my sleepyhead,
Guiding my dreams like a warm loaf of bread.
With giggles and grins, I roll to the side,
In the realm of blankets, I take endless pride.

So here in this haven, my musings do sway,
Like a sleepy sloth, I'm snuggled all day.
What else can be pondered, what nonsense awaits?
Oh, sweet lullabies, I abide by your fates.

A Cocoon of Comfort

Wrapped in my sheets, I'm a burrito divine,
Binge-watching penguins while sipping on wine.
Each waddle a mystery, each flap a delight,
In my cozy cocoon, I'm winning the night.

The world's out there spinning, but I'm stuck in here,
Debating if daylight could ever seem clear.
Should I build a pillow tall as a tower?
Or just snuggle deeper, claiming my power?

Snacks on the nightstand line up like a train,
Popcorn, chips, and candy, oh what a gain!
As I chew and I ponder, giggles I stow,
What's the meaning of life? I don't really know.

But here in my fortress, it's more of a feast,
Comfort's my kingdom, fatigue's my least.
So let thoughts of the world drift far, far away,
In my cozy cocoon, I'll forever stay.

Navigating the Nook of Night

In the nook of the night, where my dreams take their course,
I sail through soft clouds, propelled by a horse.
The moon drips with laughter, stars twinkle with glee,
What will tomorrow bring? It's a mystery!

I bounce on my mattress like a kangaroo,
While daydreaming about a grand pirate crew.
Under covers I squirm, an explorer at heart,
Collecting my thoughts like a treasure map chart.

Do I conquer a kingdom or dine with a troll?
As I feast on potato chips, I'm in control!
Each little snack a delight to behold,
In this nook of the night, my laughter is bold.

So let's toast to the night and its whimsical cheer,
With a mouthful of candy, I've got nothing to fear.
In the softness of silence, I'll hum and I'll sway,
Navigating my dreams, I'm quite here to stay.

Beneath Sheets of Hidden Wonders

In a fortress of cotton, I lay and I dream,
Pillow fights with thoughts that are never quite seen.
Monsters of laundry, they dance on the floor,
While I seek the wisdom behind the closed door.

A snack on the nightstand, my trusty terrain,
Every crumb's a treasure in this cozy domain.
Reclining like royalty, I ponder my fate,
What if the remote is the key to my state?

Pajama-clad hero, I brave the long night,
With dreams taking shapes, I prepare for the flight.
Outside, the world spins, but I'm snug and confined,
In the realm of my blankets, enlightenment's blind.

So here's to the laughter, the antics of sleep,
Where shadows of nonsense in my slumber do leap.
Under sheets of soft wonder, my thoughts take a ride,
In the kingdom of snoozes, my spirits abide.

The Canvas of a Restless Mind

My bed's an art gallery of hopes and some fears,
Each wrinkle a memory, each crease holds my tears.
I paint with my pillow, designs bold and bright,
Creating a masterpiece in the hush of night.

Cereal for dinner is now a fine dish,
Best served while wrapped in a blanket—my wish.
As I sketch out my plans with a spoon in my hand,
A canvas of chaos—who would understand?

The clock plays a prank, I swear it must mock,
Ticking away dreams like an old, naughty clock.
In the silence, I pause, wonder why I'm awake,
As eagles of nonsense dive into my cake.

Yet in this soft chaos, I think and I laugh,
Concocting absurdities, my own little path.
A true work of art, with humor and jest,
In the canvas of bedtime, I'm truly blessed.

Journeying Through Fabricated Realms

Under stars of my ceiling, I voyage so far,
Adventuring boldly, my own little star.
With plushy companions, I travel through space,
In pajamas of justice, I battle the haste.

An empire of pillows, my throne on the bed,
I reign over kingdoms, where dreams dare to tread.
With laughter as my sword, I conquer the night,
In realms that are fluffy, my spirit takes flight.

Unicorns and dragons dance under my sheets,
In this fabricated land, my imagination greets.
Each flip of the blanket, a twist of the tale,
A journey of giggles on a magical trail.

So here in the soft, I wander and roam,
My bed's the great ship that sails me back home.
These journeys of whimsy keep joy at my side,
For happiness found is a wonderful ride.

Echoes of Solitude Under Covers

In the cocoon of my blanket, I find my own crew,
Whispering secrets that only I knew.
Echoes of laughter against bedroom walls,
I giggle at shadows, my mind freely sprawls.

A fortress of solitude, yet no one's around,
With each rustle of sheets, a new joke is found.
I dive into silence, a clammy embrace,
With pillows as partners, I laugh at the space.

Why venture outside when my bed's a delight?
I launch into battles with invisible fright.
Each sneeze sends a message to those passing by,
"Do not disturb me, I'm touching the sky!"

So here in my haven, I cherish it all,
The echoes of solitude, my personal hall.
Living the dream in this comfy cocoon,
I'll nap through the troubles, awakening soon.

Echoing Softness

In a cocoon of blankets tight,
Pillow fights with shadows bright,
Chasing dreams, a silly quest,
Snuggled up, I find my rest.

Hamster wheels spin in my head,
While visions dance, and giggles spread,
Socks that vanish, lost in play,
Tangled thoughts drift far away.

A kingdom ruled by plush and fluff,
Where life is soft and never tough,
Morning light, a sneaky thief,
Stealing moments of pure relief.

As I roll from side to side,
My secret stash, I will not hide,
Chocolate wrappers, crumbs galore,
My little joys, a hidden store.

In the Quietude of Cotton Dreams

Under covers, I cocoon,
With my thoughts and a spoon,
Counting sheep that wear a crown,
In this realm, I won't drown.

Frogs in pajamas jump with glee,
Pillow clouds are home to me,
Snoozing giants in pajama fights,
Laughing softly into the nights.

My alarm clock beeps like it's insane,
But I'm in a dance with fluffy brain,
Dreaming of cake and the world's best stew,
While my slippers join the two-step too!

Cotton dreams that make me sigh,
Where the wildest thoughts can fly,
Waking up is such a bore,
Why can't I just snooze some more?

Unraveling Quiet Contemplations

Beneath the stars, my mind will roam,
In this fortress made of foam,
Questioning if socks have feelings,
As I ponder funny ceilings.

Cuddled deep like a burrito,
Debating life's mysteries, oh so slow,
Are the snack crumbs a sign of bliss?
Or just evidence of a late night kiss?

The cat looks on with knowing gaze,
As I lose myself in this soft maze,
Plotting schemes of fun and cheer,
Building castles of pillows near.

Every snore is a symphony,
As I reign in this kingdom free,
With dreams that turn my thoughts to play,
In the silliness of a sleepy sway.

Under Cover of Moonlight

Whispers of dreams swirl all around,
Under blankets, I am crowned,
Moonlight tickles my lazy feet,
This fuzzy throne can't be beat.

Blanket forts rise like great towers,
As I lounge, lost in the hours,
With a book that's just half-read,
I venture on, still snug in bed.

Are the snacks I hide in here,
A treasure chest or cause for fear?
With crumbs to share, I laugh and shout,
In this lair, there's no doubt.

Starlit giggles burst like bubbles,
Visions of dancing, silly troubles,
As night wraps snug around my dreams,
Life is funny, or so it seems!

Deep Thoughts Under Down

Beneath the fluff, I ponder things,
Like why my sock still has no mate.
Is pondering under covers wise?
Or just a way to procrastinate?

A taco truck in dreams appears,
With guacamole on the side.
But when I wake, it's toast I have,
Oh, where'd my tasty dreams abide?

I think of life and toast and spread,
And all the crumbs beneath my sheets.
If I could solve the world's great woes,
It all might just begin with eats!

So here I lie, my brain in gears,
While cats plot world domination.
I'll stay wrapped up in cozy warmth,
And let them make the big decisions.

Navigating the Spaces Between

Between the pillows, thoughts do roam,
Where silly dreams begin to dwell.
A pirate ship or cake so sweet,
Oh wait, it's just my snoring swell!

The morning light can be so rude,
It mocks my tranquil, cozy cocoon.
I swear I just fell into sleep,
Now daybreak's here too soon!

I wonder if the cat agrees,
As he steals my favorite spot.
His purring thoughts just fill the air,
While I remain a lazy lot.

In battles fought with sheets and dreams,
I traverse through my kingdom's space.
Though kingdoms won't pay taxes, say,
I'd conquer them from this warm place!

Tender Tranquility

In the land of blankets, I find peace,
As visions drift like clouds above.
With snacks beside me, life's a breeze,
This cozy fortress I truly love.

The world can wait, it's not so dire,
Outside, they're rushing; it's all a blur.
But here in my space, I'll conspire,
To unravel who stole my last burr!

I craft philosophies with snacks,
A donut circle, life's a ring.
Perhaps I'll solve the universe,
While cuddled in this duvet's cling!

Each thought flows gently like warm tea,
While giggles bubble in the air.
I'll stay here, forever carefree—
A scholar in my blanket lair!

The Nest of Night's Queries

In this nest, the questions bloom,
Like where's my phone? I need to call.
Or is that chocolate on my shirt?
Mysterious stains abound through it all!

With every creak of bedpost's wood,
I muse of wonder and of jest.
Did I really eat that whole pie?
I'll stick with dreams; they're for the best!

The shadows dance like ghosts of doubt,
While I ponder just what's for lunch.
If only I could twiddle about,
And serve my late-night snack with a punch!

But now I snicker, muse, and lie,
In a fort of fluff, so snug and tight.
In dreams, I'm bold, but then I sigh,
Tomorrow brings the morning light!

Dawning Realizations

In blankets tight, I plot my schemes,
With coffee dreams and chocolate beams.
The world outside can take its time,
While I conduct my sleepy rhyme.

The pillow speaks in muffled tones,
While I consider my old bones.
Is there a purpose in snooze?
Or just reruns of my afternoon blues?

The cat brings wisdom, perched so high,
In dreams of fish, he starts to fly.
I ponder life's profoundest jest,
Is sloth a virtue or just a pest?

Yet every yawn reveals a clue,
Perhaps nap time is where we grew.
I rise to greet the day ahead,
But first, one last hug with my bed.

The Threadbare Journey

My sheets, once bright, now dull and frayed,
Hold whispers of dreams that never played.
The quest for meaning, who needs that?
When there's a sandwich on my mat!

With crumbs as my loyal questing knights,
I navigate these blurry heights.
The pillow fortress, my trusted friend,
In slumber parties that never end.

The clock ticks on, but I remain,
In this haven of soft, my brain's domain.
Why chase the sun when I can snore?
In this tiny world, I ask for more.

So here I lay, a sage in dreams,
Deferring plans, it's not as it seems.
Between two worlds, I often tread,
But first, let's cuddle just a bit, instead.

An Odyssey in Dreamscapes

In realms of fluff, I take my flight,
On cotton clouds, from day to night.
Exploring depths of cozy lands,
With nap-time maps in sleepy hands.

Here, shadows morph into silly things,
Like talking chairs and dancing swings.
Each whimsy grand, a soft embrace,
As laughter echoes in this space.

The quest for snacks is never far,
I roll for chips, that's who we are!
A drowsy hero on a quest,
With every snooze, I'm truly blessed.

In dreamscapes wild, I hold my shield,
Against the day, that strange battlefield.
Till sleep retreats and light breaks through,
I'll argue with my dreams anew.

The Fabric of Restful Inquiry

In soft recesses, I take my stand,
With fluff for armor, dreams unplanned.
The universe hums a lazy tune,
As I seek joy before noon.

Quilted thoughts weave in and out,
A tapestry of whims, no doubt.
The mysteries of life, I ponder still,
While drowsy giggles fit my will.

With snuggly thoughts that start to blend,
I find my peace where puzzles end.
What's life without this tender pause?
A sleepy sage with quirky laws.

So raise a toast to restful nights,
To couches warm and pillow fights.
Here in my haven, I find delight,
In the fabric of sleeps that feel just right.

Nighttime Musings

Under stars, my thoughts take flight,
Pillow fights with dreams at night.
Sneaky snacks hide 'neath the bed,
Whispers of blankets, visions spread.

Silly socks dance in moon's beam,
Tickling toes, oh what a dream!
Monsters of laundry loom with dread,
Yet I'm the king, in my blanket shed.

A pizza slice guides my quest,
Crumbs of wisdom are the best.
Each laugh echoes soft and bright,
As I ponder life's silly plight.

In this fort of cozy delight,
Every giggle feels just right.
Wrapped in warmth, I find my grin,
In the chaos, I spin and spin.

Beneath the Quilt of Reflection

Under layers, I plot and scheme,
Pillow forts inspire the dream.
Fuzzy thoughts float like a cloud,
Each giggle muffled, soft, and loud.

Socks with holes tell tales of old,
Blanket monsters, brave and bold.
My teddy guards my nighttime fun,
In this fortress, I am the one.

Midnight snacks, the crunch divine,
Chocolate whispers, 'You'll be fine!'
In the shadows, secrets dwell,
But here, they're just a story to tell.

Each snore is music to my ears,
The softest symphony calms my fears.
As dreams parade, I flip and spin,
In this quilted realm, I always win.

Solace Amongst Soft Sheets

In cotton realms where chuckles hide,
Beneath the sheets, my dreams collide.
Laughter bubbles, a rhythmic sound,
As midnight snacks are often found.

Quirky thoughts in cozy nooks,
Worming through my bedtime books.
Each page cracked tells stories true,
Of silly socks and things I knew.

The alarm clock grins, a sneaky foe,
But I'll win the snooze game, you know!
The softest sheets, my trusted crew,
Guard my dreams and waffle goo.

With every snore, a comic beat,
In cozy chaos, life feels sweet.
Wrapped in laughter, love, and cheer,
This comfy kingdom holds me near.

The Silent Sanctuary

In silence wrapped, I claim my throne,
Pillow angling just for fun.
Quirky dreams begin to sprout,
With each sleepy yawn, I'm out!

Monsters hide beneath the sheets,
But wait, they're just my missing treats!
Silly whispers glide in air,
In nighttime's grasp, I shed my care.

The clock strikes twelve, a gentle tease,
For laughs do echo, soft as breeze.
Snuggled tight, my thoughts take flight,
Creating tales 'til morning light.

So here beneath my fortress bright,
I find the humor in the night.
In fluffy solace, I shall remain,
As dreams and giggles comb my brain.

Reflections in a Sea of Fabric

In the folds of my blanket, a journey begins,
I ponder life's questions while snuggling in spins.
Is my snack stash enough for this deep contemplation?
Or shall I close my eyes, embrace hibernation?

The pillows conspire to pull me away,
Whispers of comfort beg me to stay.
I dream of adventures, of lands far and wide,
Yet here in my fortress, I choose to abide.

Tangled in sheets like a ship's sturdy sail,
I float on the surface, where laughter prevails.
If wisdom is found in the fluff of a quilt,
Then surely my comfort is where my heart's built.

So pass me the popcorn and turn off the light,
My kingdom of cushions is where I take flight.
With giggles abound, and my stillness in check,
I'll search for enlightenment, what the heck!

Lost in Untangled Thoughts

Nestled away in my fortress of fluff,
Thoughts swirl like socks in a dryer—quite tough.
Should I ponder the cosmos or simply nap?
Decisions are tricky when wrapped in a wrap!

Beneath the soft covers, the world feels so bright,
Every whim, every worry, drifts out of sight.
I contemplate breakfast—it surely must wait,
When the adventure is finding my lost sock's fate.

As shadows grow longer, and dreams start to creep,
I wonder if wisdom grows better with sleep.
In laughter, I find that I'm still wide awake,
While thoughts in my head play a jazzy old shake.

Yet, wrapped up in comfort, I giggle and snore,
Each hiccup of thought makes me love it much more.
Who knew the best journey is bound in this bed?
With laughter and pillows, I'll rest my bright head!

Repose and Reflection

Under the covers, my safe little zone,
I rest and reflect, on topics alone.
Should I solve the world's problems or just snooze?
The humor of it all? I cannot refuse!

Muffled by pillows that cradle my head,
I ponder the 'why' from the warmth of my bed.
In this cozy cocoon, with a snack by the side,
I giggle at life, watch my worries subside.

A flash of old movies twirls in my mind,
Like a dance on the carpet, it's casual, unkind.
The cat gives a yawn, as if saying, "Oh please,
You've got the best seat; I'll join with such ease."

So here I shall linger, in laughter's embrace,
Where deep thoughts and giggles both settle in place.
With dreams filled with mischief, I aim to transgress,
Why leave my warm chamber? I'm truly blessed!

Clarity Caught in a Cradle

In a cradle of comfort, my thoughts start to roam,
Am I wiser than yesterday? Doubtful—just foam.
With a snack in the night and Netflix on queue,
I ponder the universe over hot cocoa too!

While the world seems so loud outside my warm lair,
I ponder big questions in my fluffy chair.
Does chocolate bring clarity? Perhaps, or is it,
Just a clever excuse to loll about, sit?

My pillow's soft wisdom insists on repose,
It whispers such secrets, as each moment slows.
In the folds of my blanket, adventure is sweet,
In laughter, I find wisdom; it's my little treat.

So here's to the night and the joy it bequeaths,
To the giggles that brighten as the mind weaves.
Caught in a cradle of dreams and of cheer,
I'll toast to my comfort; raise a glass of good beer!

Pillows Holding Secrets Untold

In the quiet realm where dreams reside,
My pillow's whispers, they cannot hide.
Beneath the fluff and feathery mound,
Is a treasure chest of thoughts unbound.

I ponder life while snug and warm,
As my blanket shields from the outside storm.
Each crease and fold, a story spun,
Of last night's antics, oh what fun!

With snacks and crumbs tucked right in,
A pillow fight—a silly win.
Did I really wear my socks to bed?
Or just dreamt of them inside my head?

In midnight's glow, I laugh with glee,
At the oddities that come to me.
Oh secrets held in this cozy night,
Are they just dreams or truths in flight?

A Sanctuary of Lost Reflections

In the fortress of sheets, I plot and scheme,
With half a thought, I'm a daytime dream.
The fluff reflects my joyful frown,
Who knew a bed could wear a crown?

The alarm clock sneers from the bedside shelf,
While I debate the merits of 'get-up' vs 'self.'
Pajamas marked with coffee stains,
Tell tales of lazy, glorious gains.

I sat up once, was it a lifetime ago?
Or just a quick snack break, I don't really know.
Time melts like ice cream in the sun,
In this sanctuary of lost fun.

With dreams piled high and pillows askew,
I giggle softly at thoughts that ensue.
The comfort of here can't be dismissed,
Am I growing wiser? Or just too blissed?

Slumber's Embrace and Silent Queries

Wrapped in blankets, I drift and sway,
Questions buzzing, like bees at play.
If I count the sheep, will sleep come faster?
Or does it matter, if dreams are a disaster?

At midnight, the ceiling has much to say,
With patterns and shadows, they dance and sway.
Is the key to life hidden in the fluff?
Or just the fact that chocolate's enough?

The pillow so plush, it cradles my grin,
As I ponder where my last snack's been.
If slumber is sweet, what of this fuss?
Could it be life's all about the plus?

In cozy depths, I muse and jest,
With every snore, I feel so blessed.
For in this space of jest and cheer,
I find my answers hiding near.

In the Nest of Quiet Contemplation

In a nest of blankets, I softly lie,
Watching the world through my sleepy eye.
Did I leave the stove on, or was it a dream?
My mind tends to wander, or so it would seem.

Fluffing my pillows, I sift through my plans,
With a taco in mind, yes, life understands.
The plush cave of comfort is where I explore,
What weird thing I'll think of next, that's for sure!

What if the cat thinks I'm merely a snack?
Or the socks on the floor are staging an attack?
In layers of coziness, thoughts take flight,
Each chuckle and grin brings cheer to the night.

As I nestle deep, the cosmos seems clear,
In this fortress I've built, there's nothing to fear.
For amidst pillows and dreams, I'm never alone,
The laughter in bed sometimes feels like home.

Moonlit Meditations

Under the sheets, I take my stand,
Pillows like clouds, soft and grand.
Dreams fill the room, a quirky parade,
With socks as my soldiers, I'm ready to wade.

Pillows speak secrets, head full of fluff,
Whispers of laughter, just barely enough.
The cat joins my quest, with a pounce and a grin,
In this nightly realm, we dive right in.

Lurking beneath is the box of old toys,
Distant romances and forgotten joys.
Jumbled together, like soup on the stove,
Each spoonful a memory, the tales that I rove.

With every snore, the world fades away,
The comfort of linens, a grand cabaret.
On this wild ride, I can't help but grin,
Though I can't find my keys, let the fun begin!

Comfort's Unraveling

In the cozy nook where I plot and scheme,
Socks on a mission, as part of my dream.
Wrestling with blankets, I plan my escape,
Breakfast in bed? Oh, that's pure drape!

The alarm clock giggles, just out of sight,
It knows I won't rise till the morning light.
With crumbs on my shirt and a grin on my face,
I invent new reasons to claim this space.

A rogue pillow fights for the top of my head,
Guarding my thoughts like a fuzzy-furred thread.
It knows too much, with its feathers all frayed,
Together we scheme, a soft escapade!

As dawn tiptoes in, I curl up with glee,
Wrapped in comfort, just my socks and me.
In the theater of dreams, we're the brightest stars,
Who cares if I'm late for my brunch at the bars?

Threads of Wandering Thoughts

Twisted in sheets, like a pretzel, I lay,
Pondering pizza or salad today.
With music of snoring, a rhapsody grand,
I'm conducting my brain with a sleepy hand.

Each thread of my thoughts dancing 'round in the night,
Waltzing with shadows, oh what a sight!
The clock rolls its eyes, I chuckle and sigh,
As I question the meaning of why and of why?

Curled with my teddy, a confidant true,
We discuss the universe, the color of blue.
Imaginary friends with their whimsical ways,
Turn every night into a joyous malaise.

But here comes the rooster, all loud and proud,
My cuddly cocoon, no longer allowed.
Yet in this soft bubble of laughter and cheer,
I'll take today's challenges with my teddy held near.

The Sanctuary of Sleep

Welcome to my fortress, the kingdom of z's,
Where socks are my subjects, and I am the breeze.
Draped in a cocoon of comfort so deep,
I rule this realm, embracing my sleep.

The walls made of pillows, the floor is a sea,
Of laundry and laughter, come hang out with me!
Bears and old movies, they chatter away,
In this muffled haven, we frolic and play.

A flicker of humor, I tickle the light,
As dreams turn to giggles, from day into night.
Here I craft stories, some silly, some meek,
Beneath cozy layers, hilarity speaks.

With dawn creeping in, I bask in the glow,
Waving goodbye to my subjects, so slow.
But the tales of the night, they'll echo and swell,
In this sanctuary, we've built quite a shell!

Between the Threads

Amidst the pillows, dreams do spin,
A sock goes missing, where's it been?
Jumbled thoughts in cozy fluff,
Inside this fort, it's just enough.

Sheets are tangled like a pretzel bite,
Chasing whispers of the night.
Muffins twirl in the head's parade,
All while the cat plots a grand charade.

Waking up feels like a quest,
For coffee's warmth, I'd trade the rest.
Conversations dance on sleepy lips,
As cereal dives in milky ships.

Buried within this quilted maze,
Life feels like a lazy maze.
With humor dressed in cotton threads,
May I stay here, where joy spreads?

A Soul Awaits

Beneath the sheets, a giggle stirs,
As dreams collide with gentle purrs.
A wandering mind on a fluffy ride,
    Teddy bears as trusty guides.

Socks debate their mismatched fate,
    Like tiny ships that can't gyrate.
Between the snore and morning sun,
The chase for cheer has just begun.

Tucked in close with warm delight,
The world reduced to a pillow fight.
In this space where time stands still,
    I ponder life, with utmost thrill.

A reason found in every laugh,
On this bed, I write my path.
With blankets wrapped like loving arms,
    Life is sweeter with goofy charms.

A Haven of Thought and Daydreams

Here in my fortress, thoughts parade,
Twinkling like stars, each like a grade.
Pillow forts, where nothings clash,
My worries slip and quietly dash.

A rogue crumb recounts last night's feast,
While morning calls, where joy has ceased.
Do I brave the fridge like a right champ?
Or stay wrapped in this wooly lamp?

My blanket speaks in whispers low,
Of silly tales and a cheeky crow.
With every giggle shared with the dawn,
I ride on clouds, just to yawn.

This cushioned realm, my cozy retreat,
Where wisdom bends but won't admit defeat.
Here's to the sunshine peeking through,
Finding glee in this laughter stew.

Finding Clarity in the Warm Embrace

The morning sun taps on my door,
Time for thoughts to start their war.
In the embrace of feathered chill,
I ponder life, perchance to thrill.

The bed, my mate, in fabric tight,
Keeps my dreams close in flight.
What's out there beyond this fluff?
Do I really want to know, or bluff?

Puzzle pieces dance in rumpled sheets,
With every yawn, adventure greets.
A sneeze escapes, the dust-bunnies rise,
Chasing laughter under sleepy skies.

Intrigued by tales my mind conceives,
I marinate in jumbled leaves.
To laugh at life, just take a peek,
In fabric soft, we find our cheek.

Drifting Through Clouds of Contemplation

Floating in dreams, a cozy spree,
While rabbits hop through thoughts of tea.
A bumblebee buzzes by my toe,
Whispering secrets about the show.

Underneath, the cat claims the throne,
As I muse alone, with a snore as my drone.
Sock puppets wave from the laundry's lair,
In this world, there's joy to spare.

With marshmallow clouds, I sketch a scene,
Of wild adventures, and dips in a stream.
The blanket's embrace feels like a hug,
While thoughts slip out, like a lovebug.

Every giggle brings light to the space,
In this crazy dance, we find our grace.
So here I'll dwell, crafting my verse,
With a grin that knows, the world's diverse.

The Embrace of Nightly Reverie

Blankets snug, a fortress tight,
The world outside fades into night.
Pillow mountains, soft and round,
Adventure waits where dreams are found.

Socks mismatched, a fashion spree,
Dreams of glory—who needs to pee?
Dancing shadows on the wall,
In my kingdom, I stand tall.

The ceiling fan spins tales so bold,
Of daring feats and treasures gold.
But first, I munch on midnight cake,
For freedom's sweet, make no mistake!

With yawns as weapons, I will slay,
The dragons of my busy day.
In this realm, I rule supreme,
A true monarch of pillow dreams.

Beneath the Canopy of Introspection

Nestled deep 'neath cotton skies,
I ponder life with sleepy eyes.
Why do socks conspire to flee?
In dreams, they dance—wild and free!

The clock ticks softly, mocking me,
While thoughts roam wild like bumblebees.
Blanket forts and secret quests,
In my mind, I am the best!

Teddy bears my loyal knights,
Guarding kingdoms through the nights.
Their fuzzy ears hear all my woes,
And fuel my laughter as it grows.

Oh, to be a pillow prince,
In fluffy realms where laughter spins.
I'll conquer sleep, just one more hour,
Before reality regains its power.

Woven Whispers of the Mind

As night creeps in, the whispers start,
My brain's a web, a tangled art.
Why did I enter this rabbit hole?
Did I forget to pay the toll?

In cozy corners of my thought,
A distant echo of what I sought.
Why is the fridge calling my name?
At 2 AM, it's such a shame!

Cuddled up like a burrito tight,
I plot world domination—what a sight!
But first, the quest for snacks begins,
A noble way to earn my wins.

With laughter bubbling in my chest,
What am I doing, you may jest?
In slumber's grip, I take my stand,
The funniest dreams are always planned.

The Hearth of Hypnos

At the edge of a dream, I sit and stew,
Wrapped in warmth, my thoughts accrue.
Does cheese really belong on pie?
These queries haunt as I aim to fly.

Monsters hide beneath my bed,
But they're just dreams inside my head!
With laughter, I resolve to tease,
A tickle fight with phantoms, please!

Mismatched sheets, a vibrant sight,
Roll around till morning light.
As shadows play their nightly game,
I proudly claim my silly fame.

With each yawn, my mind takes flight,
Filling pages with pure delight.
May this fond laughter be my guide,
As I drift down the dreamscape slide.

Restful Rambles in Lazy Light

In the cocoon, I spin and twirl,
Dreams of pizza make my head swirl.
The blanket fortress all around me,
Snuggled tight, I'm wild and free.

A sock rebellion, one lost shoe,
The couch calls out, 'Oh hey, it's you!'
Pillow fights with thoughts so cute,
A languid dance in fuzzy boots.

Doughnuts giggle from the fridge,
Whispers of snacks tempt me to pledge.
I'll conquer my hunger - one more bite,
As the sun snoozes, dimming the light.

Every snore, a sweet serenade,
In this bazaar of dreams, I wade.
Laughter spills from slumbering lips,
In my napping world, reality slips.

Cradled in the Echoes

Waves of comfort wash over me,
While the cat claims my foot - oh, what glee!
Tickle the pillows, the laughter flows,
In this sleepy realm, anything goes.

The ticking clock mocks my slow pace,
As I chase shadows — in this soft space.
Napping while the world runs around,
Outline of dreams in a cozy mound.

Muffin crumbs in my hair suffice,
For biscuit bags filled with cat's advice.
Through this cushiony haze I glide,
Cradled in echoes where secrets hide.

A gentle sigh, a contented croon,
While visions of sugar plum fairies swoon.
Lost in the whirl of a lazy land,
With a chocolate bar snug in my hand.

The Comforting Gaze of the Ceiling

The ceiling's got stories, it winks and beams,
In this lazy haven, I drift into dreams.
Dust bunnies gathering like an old crew,
In laughter we share, a sweet rendezvous.

Paint stains and whirls, a masterpiece seen,
I laugh with the light, caught in the sheen.
A distant echo — who tickled my toes?
In this warm snuggle, the fun only grows.

The charm of the past, like a playful tease,
Each crack a tale, every flake my ease.
Hours stretch like taffy, golden and sweet,
Oh, the magic of bed — where time meets defeat.

I dance with the shadows, laid back in glee,
In this soft whimsical place, just me and me.
Wrapped in the comfort, a cozy refrain,
Every giggle a ticket to silly again.

The Peaceful Pilgrimage

A journey begins with a pillow in hand,
Map of the duvet, my cozy land.
With snacks as my compass, I wander inside,
In the sea of my quilt, I take a ride.

Feet tucked in edges, bright colors collide,
Each wrinkle a path where my dreams overlap wide.
Pillow forts rise like towers of cheer,
In this sacred space, I hold treasure near.

Sweet stars above with a wink and a nod,
As popcorn clouds float on the dreams I prod.
With every soft giggle, I trace a new line,
In this expedition, everything's fine.

So here I reside in this snug little zone,
Where wishes take flight, and I'm never alone.
In my peaceful pilgrimage, laughter unfurls,
The world waits outside for the next silly twirl.

Blankets of Benevolent Thoughts

Underneath this cozy layer,
Where socks lose their pairs,
I ponder life's odd treasure,
Like lost candy and old hairs.

The cat takes up my side,
Claiming warmth, it's true,
While I'm stuck with the thought,
"Is the fridge full of stew?"

Wiggling toes in blissful haze,
The refrigerator hums,
In this haven, crazy days,
Feel as light as my crumbs.

Each wrinkle holds a wonder,
Like distant distant lands,
With snacks in nearby slumber,
And dreams served in bedpans.

Pillows as Portals

My pillows, soft as clouds,
Whisper tales of sleepy lore,
Inviting me to hide away,
From chores I can't ignore.

Cereal's caught in my hair,
A relic from last night's fun,
Yet in this plush throne of fluff,
I'm a champion on the run.

Every yawn a ticket bought,
To realms where jellybeans grow,
With unicorns who love to dance,
And socks that never blow.

I snooze to dodge reality,
And slide by the day's demand,
In a world made of cotton,
Where bedtime's always grand!

Respite in the Realm of Dreams

In this fortress snug and tight,
Adventures wait, unseen yet bold,
I ride on waves of marshmallow fluff,
While the outside world grows cold.

Monsters hide under the bed,
But my teddy fights them away,
With every snort and sleepy shrug,
We chase the mundane far away.

Sandwiches fly, and spoons talk back,
In this land where logic's thin,
Where pajamas are armor,
And a day's worth of laughter begins.

Then alarm bells ring, oh what a plight!
With a groan, I face the sun,
But in my heart, I cradle dreams,
Of a whimsical life full of fun.

Seeking Stillness in Softness

Nestled deep in pillow land,
Where thoughts bounce like rubber balls,
I quietly plot to understand,
Why the laundry basket calls.

Fluffy dreams and sock disputes,
Razzamatazz in every seam,
Here time stumbles on soft roots,
As I board the last train of dream.

Sipping cocoa from a mug,
While invisible spirits dance,
They tickle my sleepy mind,
And summon forth a giggle trance.

So here I'll stay, snug and tight,
Wrapped in laughs and sweet delight,
For life finds meaning, rare and fun,
In the warm embrace of undone.

Submerged in the Slow Drift of Sleep

Beneath the covers, I'm a ship,
Sailing seas of wool and fluff.
Dreams are fish that swim and flip,
Caught in currents, never tough.

The pillow's soft, a comfy shore,
Where thoughts get tangled, gently spun.
My eyelids drop, wanting more,
As snores replace a day of fun.

A wild wave of bedtime tales,
Floods my mind with laughing sights.
Pirate quests and furry snails,
Navigating through soft twilight.

But alarms will blare and I must rise,
To greet the world with sleepy eyes.

The Hidden Gems of Wool

My blanket's plush, a treasure chest,
Of quirky threads and stubby seams.
In cozy corners, I find the best,
A kingdom born from snuggly dreams.

Underneath this grand design,
I unearth jewels: bits of fluff,
Tiny toys and crumbs align,
All making comfort feel enough.

A sock that vanished? Now a scarf!
Pillows whisper secrets that jest.
In this soft realm, you'll hear my laugh,
Among the pillows, who's the best?

Where warmth and humor cozy blend,
I dive deep into my laid-back spree.

Lingering Thoughts Under the Stars

As I nestle in my cocoon,
Stars blink like eyes from a fuzzy sky,
Thoughts bounce like bunnies, oh so soon,
Cuddled whispers softly sigh.

The galaxy stretches, oh so wide,
Yet here I am, feeling quite clever.
In fluffy realms, I roam with pride,
What's better than sleep? Nothing ever!

My dreams are painted with silly brush,
Adventures that make me giggle and squeal.
Floating in dreams, oh, what a rush!
Who needs the world when you can feel?

In this sweet zone, the laughter rings,
Under a quilt of fanciful things.

Where Comfort Meets Curiosity

In this nest of fluff and warmth,
Questions bounce like popcorn flies.
What makes a cat so full of charm?
Or why do socks vanish? Oh, the highs!

Exploring realms where giggles bloom,
My covers flip like pages turned.
In these depths, I find my room,
Where every snicker is well-earned.

The mysteries of midnight snack,
Why does the blanket feel so right?
I ponder as I watch the crack,
Of dawn peeking through the night.

With sleepy eyes and playful grin,
In comfort's arms, I grin within.

Tucked Between Pages of the Soul

In the creases of my pillow, I sink,
Dreams flutter like pages, or so I think.
Pajama-clad thoughts take a whimsical flight,
While my blanket cocoon is my only delight.

Sneaky epiphanies sneak through the seams,
Tickling my mind like poorly written memes.
With every yawn, wisdom whispers so sweet,
Yet all I can muster is snacks for a treat.

Dancing dust motes wink from the light,
Their giggles echo deep into the night.
Chasing ideas like cats chase their tails,
But cozy distractions are where contentment prevails.

A universe waits in this snug little den,
I'm the captain of dreams, without need of a pen.
But if life's answers are found in my sheets,
Why do I still wonder when I'm counting my eats?

A Celestial Refuge

Nestled within my fortress of fluff,
Clouds are my neighbors, yet still, I'm stuck.
While galaxies swirl in my drifty mind,
I'm in pursuit of snacks, not answers to find.

Starlight peeks in through the curtain's embrace,
While my thoughts drift off to a chocolate cake place.
Constellations twinkle, they yell to the night,
But I just want snacks with my interstellar flight.

Cuddly UFOs made of pillows surround,
Zooming through dreams, it's silliness found.
But logic's lost in my merry retreat,
As I float on my mattress like candy on heat.

In this celestial realm where I'm ever so free,
Existential crises just can't come for tea.
Who needs answers with comfort so grand?
I'll ponder tomorrow — while munching on bran.

Soft Shadows and Silent Searches

Wrestling with shadows that dance on the wall,
Each squeaky floorboard gives secrets a call.
Whispers of purpose beckon me near,
Yet all I can hear is the fridge's cheer.

Beneath layers of blankets, I float far away,
Where questions are answered in silly ballet.
The night is a canvas, my mind a bright mess,
While my blanket brigade makes skepticism confess.

I guard my thoughts like prized jellybeans,
Yet wander through meadows of hasty daydreams.
The answers I seek seem to giggle and hide,
As I roll over, seeking comfort inside.

If meaning sprouts wings and flits like a bee,
Why does my bed feel like such a decree?
Cocooned in my layers, nothing makes sense,
But the soft hush of slumber is my loud recompense.

The Quiet Quest of Meaning

In the realm where the night mist kisses my cheek,
I seek out the wisdom that's ever so bleak.
With eyes half-closed, I ponder the fate,
But my brain hits snooze — it's far too late.

A parade of plushies hold council in gloom,
While I navigate thoughts through my dark, cozy room.
Philosophers lounge, while I ask for a snack,
And pondering life seems to lead to a quack.

Yet in this nocturnal, plain pillow fight,
Great thinkers convene under starry moonlight.
Should I rise for the answers, or stay here and slumber?
In my fortress I giggle, as joys roll and lumber.

With each cozy sigh, a dream takes its flight,
While meaning dangles just out of sight.
So here on this mattress, I laugh at the quest,
'Til the morning sun says, "You can't nap, you're a mess!"

www.ingramcontent.com/pod-product-compliance
Lightning Source LLC
Chambersburg PA
CBHW051639160426
43209CB00004B/719